Racing Cars

K.M. Daynes

Designed by Helen Edmonds
and Sam Barrett

Illustrated by Adrian Dean,
Emmanuel Cerisier and Adrian Roots
Racing cars expert: James Allen,
Formula One commentator

D0240919

Contents

Stock cars race round the Atlanta Motor Speedway, USA, in a 2009 NASCAR Sprint Cup race.

Which racing car?

Racing cars can be divided into two main types: open-wheel cars that have their wheels outside the car body and other racing cars that have their wheels below.

Open wheels

Here are the three main categories of open-wheel racing. The cars are all single seaters.

The FW32, manufactured by Williams for the 2010 Formula One season

Formula One™
• **Top speed:** 360km/h (224mph)
• **Track:** road courses and street circuits
• **Race length:** 260-310km (160-190 miles)

Indy racing

- **Top speed:** 386km/h (240mph)
- **Track:** oval circuits and road courses
- **Race length:** 240-885km
  (150-550 miles)

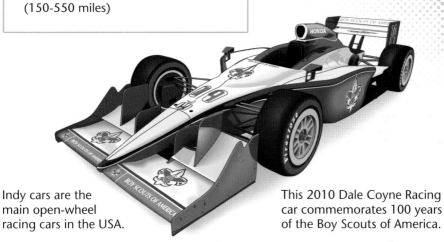

Indy cars are the main open-wheel racing cars in the USA.

This 2010 Dale Coyne Racing car commemorates 100 years of the Boy Scouts of America.

Drag racing

- **Top speed:** 530km/h (330mph)
- **Track:** short, straight sprint track
- **Race length:** 300-400 metres
  (1,000-1,320 feet)

The fastest kind of drag racing car is a top fuel dragster.

This US Army dragster has won the top fuel championship six times.

Modified road cars

Many racing cars started off as ordinary road cars. Then owners and manufacturers added better engines and improved other car parts to make them faster.

Stock car racing

- **Top speed:** 320km/h (200mph)
- **Track:** mainly oval
- **Race length:** 320-1,000km (200-600 miles)

This Home Depot stock car races in the NASCAR Sprint Cup, one of the top US race series.

Almost every part of a stock car is now handmade.

There are two main kinds of sports cars, sports prototypes and grand tourers (see page 58).

Sports prototypes, such as this Lola-Aston Martin, are purpose-built for racing.

Sports car racing

- **Top speed:** 346km/h (215mph)
- **Track:** road courses
- **Race length:** endurance races from 2.5 hours to 24 hours

Touring car racing

- **Top speed:** 225km/h (140mph)
- **Track:** road courses and street circuits
- **Race length:** short sprints to 24 hours

This Honda Civic competed in the 2010 British Touring Car Championship.

Touring cars have a standard body shell, but everything inside is modified for racing.

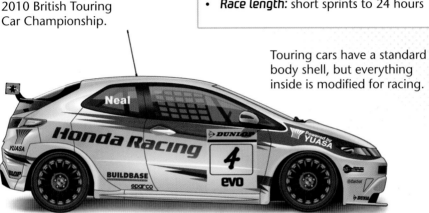

Rallying

- **Top speed:** 225km/h (140mph)
- **Track:** off-road courses or closed public roads
- **Race length:** made up of stages, each under 50km (30 miles) long

This Ford Focus WRC car won the World Rally Championship in 2006 and 2007.

Rally car modifications include improved suspension to cope with rough terrain.

Formula One™

Formula One, or F1, is the most famous kind of racing. F1 car designs have changed over the decades, since the first world championship in 1950. Here are some examples.

1950s

Alfa Romeo 159 (1950-1953)

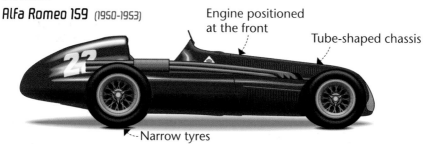

Engine positioned at the front

Tube-shaped chassis

Narrow tyres

1960s

Brabham BT20 (1966-1969)

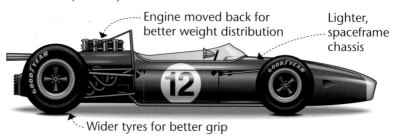

Engine moved back for better weight distribution

Lighter, spaceframe chassis

Wider tyres for better grip

1970s

Lotus 72D (1971-1975)

Rear wing

Engine

Air box to channel more air to engine

Wings added to push car onto track

Radiator moved from nose to sidepods to create wedge shape

Stronger aluminium chassis

Finding the formula

F1 is the top level of over ten formula racing series. The 'formula' is a set of rules devised for each series to make the cars more evenly matched. The formulae are updated each year and manufacturers race to create the best car...

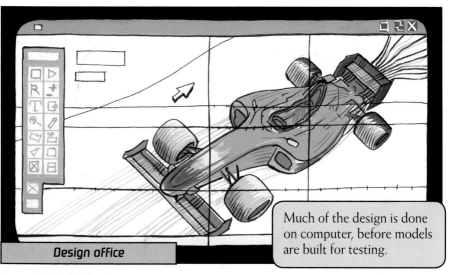

Design office

Much of the design is done on computer, before models are built for testing.

Engine workshop

The engine is mostly built by hand. It takes a technician 50 hours to make an exhaust pipe.

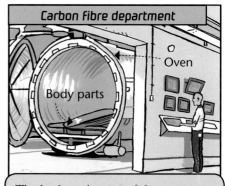

Carbon fibre department

Oven

Body parts

The body and wings of the car are made from carbon fibre. They're shaped and baked in an oven.

Mercedes GP Silver Arrow, 2010

- **Top speed:** 340km/h (211mph)
- **Engine:** V8, 750hp
- **0-100km/h (0-62mph):** 2.8s

V8 is the type of engine. 750hp is its output, measured in horsepower.

Time it takes for the car to accelerate from 0-100km/h (0-62mph) in seconds (s)

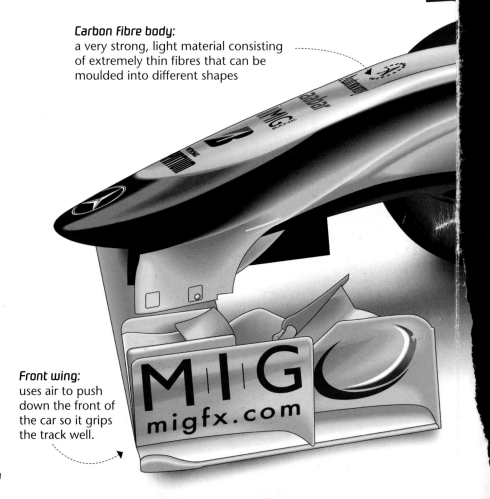

Carbon fibre body:
a very strong, light material consisting of extremely thin fibres that can be moulded into different shapes

Front wing:
uses air to push down the front of the car so it grips the track well.

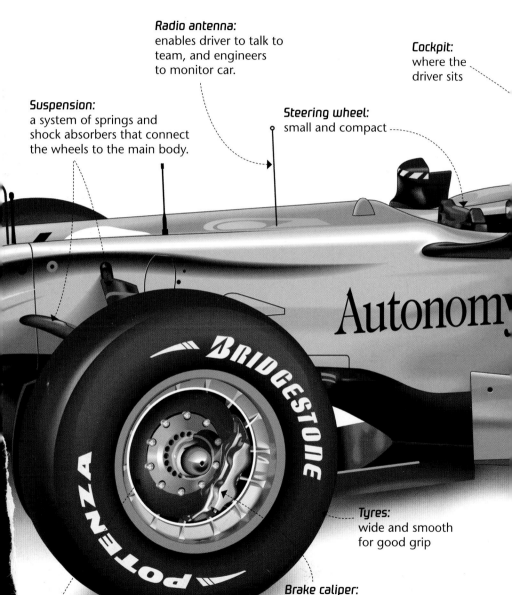

Radio antenna:
enables driver to talk to team, and engineers to monitor car.

Cockpit:
where the driver sits

Suspension:
a system of springs and shock absorbers that connect the wheels to the main body.

Steering wheel:
small and compact

Autonom

BRIDGESTONE

POTENZA

Tyres:
wide and smooth for good grip

Brake disc

Brake caliper:
slows the car down by squeezing two brake pads onto the brake disc.

The Tyrell P34 is the only six-wheeled car to have competed in an F1 race. It won the Swedish Grand Prix in 1976.

1980s
McLaren MP4-1 (1981-1983)

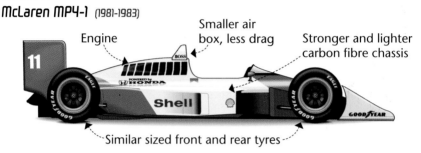

Engine

Smaller air box, less drag

Stronger and lighter carbon fibre chassis

Similar sized front and rear tyres

1990s
Williams FW18 (1996)

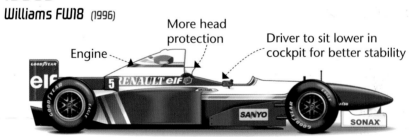

More head protection

Engine

Driver to sit lower in cockpit for better stability

2000s
Ferrari F2007 (2007)

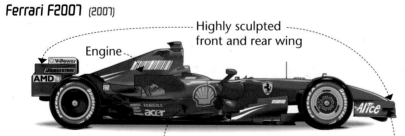

Highly sculpted front and rear wing

Engine

Streamlined sides to reduce drag

Fins added to direct airflow

Engine test bed

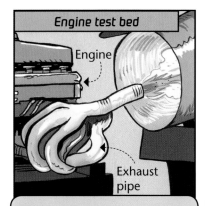

Engine

Exhaust pipe

The engine is fixed to a work top called a test bed and its performance is examined.

Wind tunnel

Half-size models of the car are exposed to strong winds to replicate how the car would behave at top speed.

Shaker rig

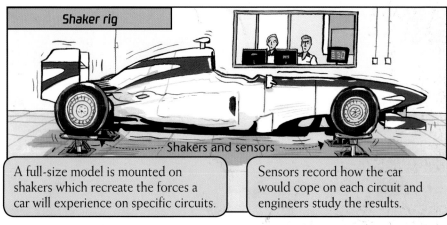

Shakers and sensors

A full-size model is mounted on shakers which recreate the forces a car will experience on specific circuits.

Sensors record how the car would cope on each circuit and engineers study the results.

Race bay

When all the design changes have been made, the final racing car is put together.

The engine

Engineers try to make the most powerful engine possible within the race rules, but the basic design is the same as in a normal car.

How engines work

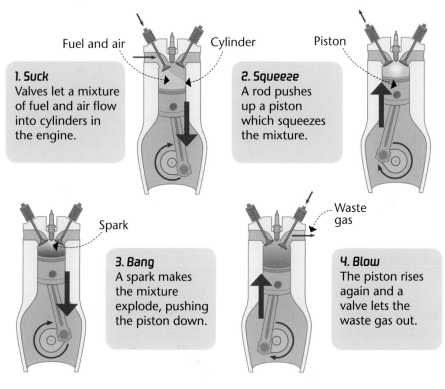

Fuel and air   Cylinder   Piston

1. Suck
Valves let a mixture of fuel and air flow into cylinders in the engine.

2. Squeeze
A rod pushes up a piston which squeezes the mixture.

Spark

3. Bang
A spark makes the mixture explode, pushing the piston down.

Waste gas

4. Blow
The piston rises again and a valve lets the waste gas out.

A key to the engine parts

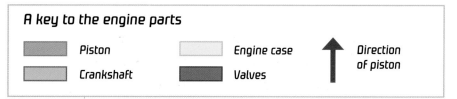

Piston

Crankshaft

Engine case

Valves

Direction of piston

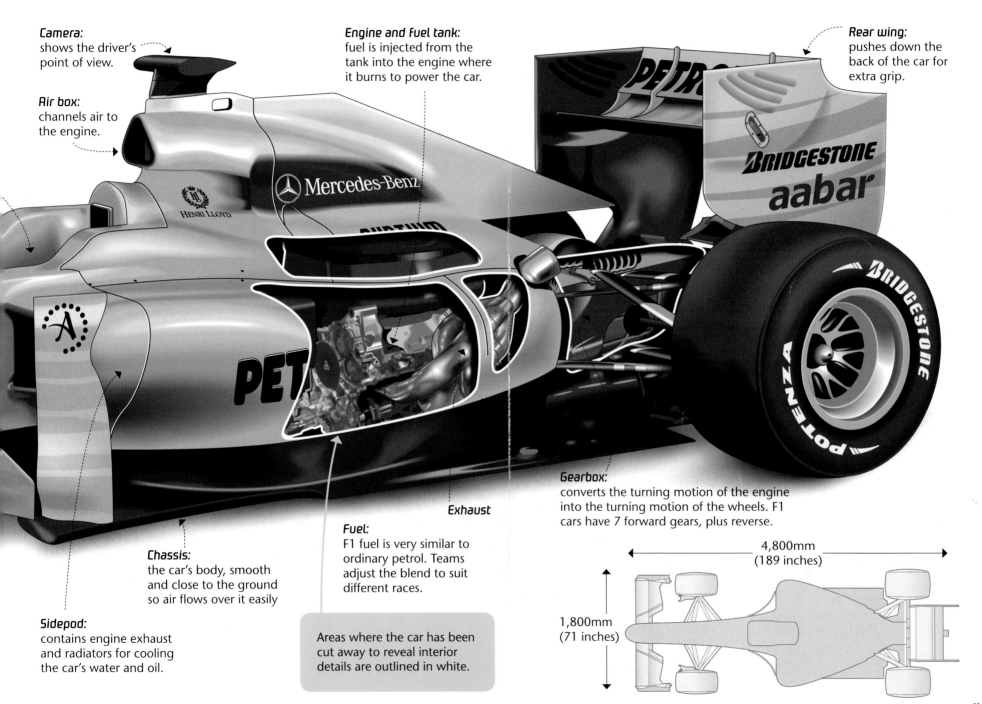

Camera:
shows the driver's point of view.

Air box:
channels air to the engine.

Engine and fuel tank:
fuel is injected from the tank into the engine where it burns to power the car.

Rear wing:
pushes down the back of the car for extra grip.

Mercedes-Benz

HENRI LLOYD

BRIDGESTONE

aabar

PETRON

PET

POTENZA

BRIDGESTONE

Chassis:
the car's body, smooth and close to the ground so air flows over it easily

Sidepod:
contains engine exhaust and radiators for cooling the car's water and oil.

Exhaust

Fuel:
F1 fuel is very similar to ordinary petrol. Teams adjust the blend to suit different races.

Areas where the car has been cut away to reveal interior details are outlined in white.

Gearbox:
converts the turning motion of the engine into the turning motion of the wheels. F1 cars have 7 forward gears, plus reverse.

4,800mm (189 inches)

1,800mm (71 inches)

Turning the wheels

The suck-squeeze-bang-blow process continues over and over again. The movement of the pistons turns the crankshaft, which then turns the drive shaft and the wheels.

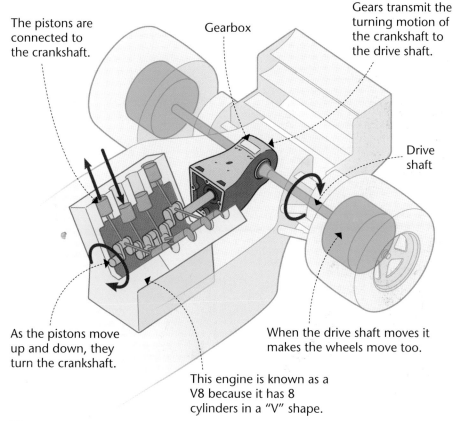

The pistons are connected to the crankshaft.

Gearbox

Gears transmit the turning motion of the crankshaft to the drive shaft.

Drive shaft

As the pistons move up and down, they turn the crankshaft.

When the drive shaft moves it makes the wheels move too.

This engine is known as a V8 because it has 8 cylinders in a "V" shape.

Horsepower

Horsepower is a unit of measurement for the output of an engine. It was introduced when engines started replacing horses as a way to power vehicles.

Streamlined shapes

Racing cars are designed with two main forces in mind: drag, the resistance caused by the air, and downforce, the downward pressure that acts on a fast-moving car.

Downforce – sucks the car onto the ground.

Drag – slows the car down.

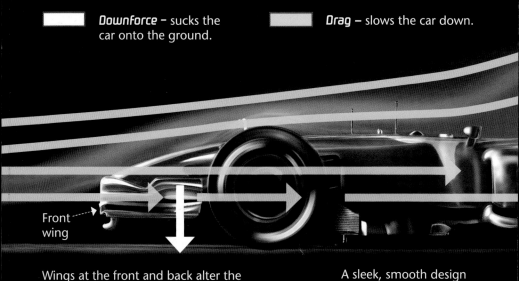

Front wing

Wings at the front and back alter the amount of drag and downforce.

A sleek, smooth design minimises drag.

Wings for twisty tracks

On twisty tracks, such as Monaco, the wings are designed to increase downforce. The car is slower but the driver has more control.

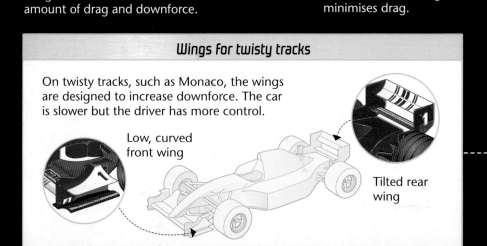

Low, curved front wing

Tilted rear wing

Why wings?

Wings on a racing car have the opposite job to wings on a plane. They are angled to stop the car lifting off the track and improve the grip of the tyres.

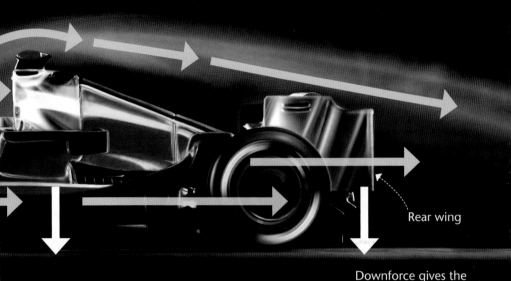

Rear wing

Downforce gives the wheels better grip.

Wings for straight tracks

On faster, straighter tracks, such as Monza, the wings are designed to reduce drag so the driver can go faster.

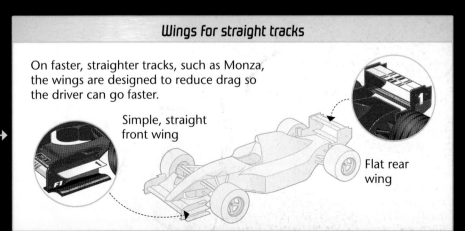

Simple, straight front wing

Flat rear wing

Brakes and boosts

F1 cars reach amazing speeds but they have such good brakes that they can stop in under three seconds. Braking quickly means the cars take less time to slow down for corners.

How the brakes work

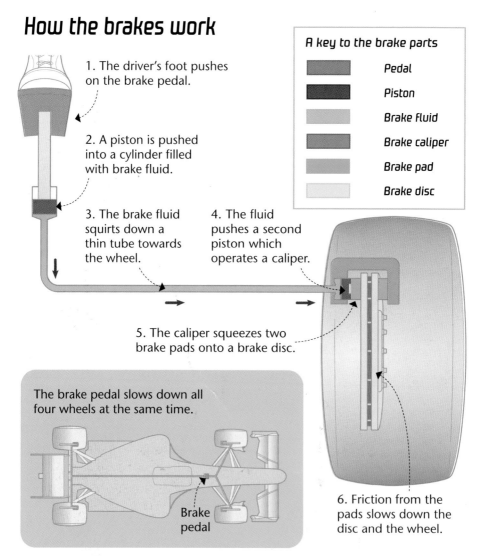

A key to the brake parts

Pedal

Piston

Brake fluid

Brake caliper

Brake pad

Brake disc

1. The driver's foot pushes on the brake pedal.

2. A piston is pushed into a cylinder filled with brake fluid.

3. The brake fluid squirts down a thin tube towards the wheel.

4. The fluid pushes a second piston which operates a caliper.

5. The caliper squeezes two brake pads onto a brake disc.

The brake pedal slows down all four wheels at the same time.

Brake pedal

6. Friction from the pads slows down the disc and the wheel.

Using brake energy

When a car brakes, its movement, known as kinetic energy, changes into heat and light energy. F1 teams can transform some of this energy into extra engine power.

The cars use a Kinetic Energy Recovery System, or KERS, to harvest and store the energy.

When the driver wants extra power, he presses a boost button on the steering wheel.

The KERS device then releases the stored energy to the engine.

Which tyres?

Tyres are the only contact a car has with the track. The more contact, the faster the car. Drivers use different kinds of tyres, depending on the weather and the race rules.

Getting a grip

Cars can slide out of control on wet tracks, so wet weather tyres are used to expel water and improve grip.

Wet weather tyres expel the water through a pattern of grooves known as a tread.

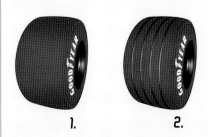 **1.**  **2.** **3.** **4.**

In dry weather	In wet weather
1. Slicks	**3. Intermediate**
• Completely smooth • Used to give the most track contact and fastest times • Two kinds: hard and soft	• Tyres with a shallow tread • Used in damp conditions to help grip
2. Grooved	**4. Wets**
• Used from 1998 to 2008 • F1 rules required at least four grooves, which made the cars slower	• Deeper tread • Used in very wet conditions to prevent skidding

Friction with the track makes the tyres warm up. If they're too cold, they can't grip the track very well. If they're too hot they can blister.

In the driving seat

It's hot, cramped and dangerous in an F1 car. The driver
sits low in the cockpit, dressed in fireproof clothes.
Everything he needs is as easy to reach as possible.

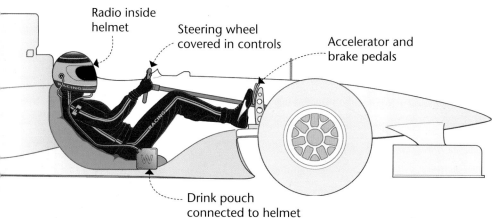

Radio inside
helmet

Steering wheel
covered in controls

Accelerator and
brake pedals

Drink pouch
connected to helmet

Driver's clothes

The clothes are made of materials such as Dupont™
Nomex® that can protect the driver from a fire for
at least 8 to 10 seconds.

Balaclava

Helmet

HANS (Head and
Neck Support) –
straps onto helmet

Overalls

Underwear

Leather gloves

Leather boots
with thin
rubber soles

Keeping in touch

The driver's radio enables him to keep in touch with his team throughout the race. He tells the team manager about any concerns.

I'm losing power. Should I make a pit stop?

We're just checking the engine monitor.

Looks like an exhaust fault. We can't fix that now.

You're fine to continue.

I'll do my best.

The team uses computers in the pit lane to monitor the car closely. They keep the driver informed and reassured throughout the race.

The steering wheel

An F1 steering wheel is the control panel for the whole car.

The five second rule

F1 safety rules state that a driver must be able to get in and out of the car in under five seconds. So steering wheels are designed to be detached and refitted quickly.

Steering wheel
• 28cm (11in) wide
• Weighs less than 1.5 kilos (3.3lbs)
• Power-assisted steering, so only a slight turn is needed for a sharp bend
• Maximum turn is ¾ of the way round

Driver Lewis Hamilton detaches the steering wheel from his F1 Vodaphone McLaren Mercedes car.

When yellow, red or blue flag is raised, lights show up here.　Speed　Gear　Lap time

Paddle lever for operating the clutch

Paddle lever for operating the gears

Buttons

- 🔴 **N/R** – neutral/reverse
- ⚪ **FLP** – moves front wing between preset positions
- ⚫ **KIL** – turns off engine
- ⚪ **OT** – uses optimum power in order to overtake
- ⚪ **BAL** – balance
- ⚪ **LIM** – limits speed for pit lane
- 🔴 **RAD** – radio
- ⚪ **CAL** – calibration of clutch
- ⚪ **DRK** – activates drink pump

Knobs

- **ENT** and **EXT** – settings for controlling entry and exit of a corner
- **FOFF** – sets alternative position for front flap
- **FNOM** – sets initial position for front flap
- **MODE** – selects timings for ignition and fuel injection
- **CLCH** – clutch
- **TRQ** – adjusts the force used to turn the crankshaft
- **MF** – multi-function dial

Grand Prix™ circuits

An F1 race is known as a Grand Prix, which means 'great prize' in French. Here are some of the most famous Grand Prix circuits.

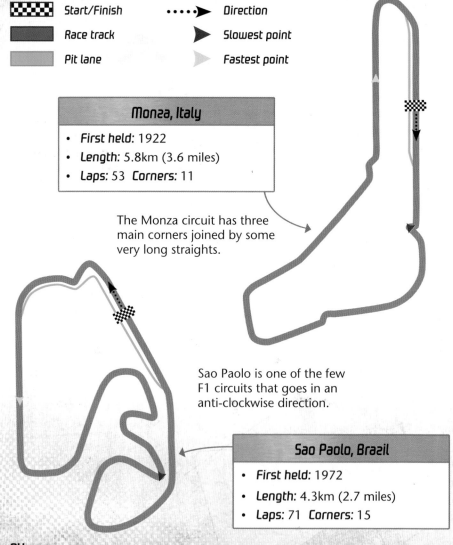

Start/Finish

Race track

Pit lane

Direction

Slowest point

Fastest point

Monza, Italy

- **First held:** 1922
- **Length:** 5.8km (3.6 miles)
- **Laps:** 53 **Corners:** 11

The Monza circuit has three main corners joined by some very long straights.

Sao Paolo is one of the few F1 circuits that goes in an anti-clockwise direction.

Sao Paolo, Brazil

- **First held:** 1972
- **Length:** 4.3km (2.7 miles)
- **Laps:** 71 **Corners:** 15

The Silverstone circuit is built on a Second World War airfield.

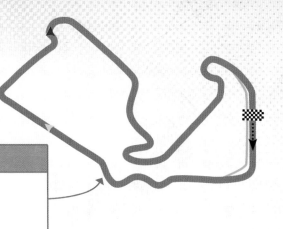

Silverstone, England

- **First held:** 1948
- **Length:** 5.9km (3.7 miles)
- **Laps:** 52 **Corners:** 18

F1's only night race takes place through the floodlit streets of Singapore.

Singapore, Southeast Asia

- **First held:** 2008
- **Length:** 5.1km (3.1 miles)
- **Laps:** 61 **Corners:** 23

Spa is F1's longest circuit. It can be raining one side and sunny the other.

Spa, Belgium

- **First held:** 1925
- **Length:** 7km (4.4 miles)
- **Laps:** 44 **Corners:** 19

Bahrain, Middle East

- **First held:** 2004
- **Length:** 6.3km (3.9 miles)
- **Laps:** 49 **Corners:** 23

Bahrain has very large run-off areas (spaces where cars can come off the track without crashing) making it one of the safest circuits in the world.

Nürburgring, Germany

- **First held:** 1984
- **Length:** 5.1km (3.2 miles)
- **Laps:** 60 **Corners:** 16

There is a much older Nürburg circuit but it's considered too dangerous for modern F1 cars.

The German Grand Prix now alternates between Nürburgring and a circuit in Hockenheim.

Shanghai, China

- **First held:** 2004
- **Length:** 5.5km (3.4 miles)
- **Laps:** 56 **Corners:** 16

The circuit shape is inspired by the first character in the Chinese name for Shanghai: 上 .

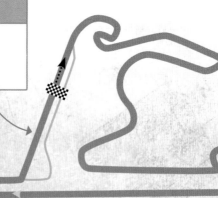

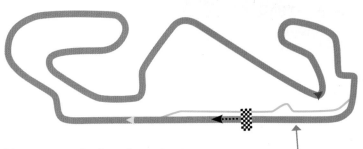

The Montreal track is built on a man-made island, in the St. Lawrence river.

Montreal, Canada

- **First held:** 1978
- **Length:** 4.4km (2.7 miles)
- **Laps:** 70 **Corners:** 12

Annual stock car and sports car races also take place on this circuit.

F1 teams use the Barcelona circuit to test their cars at the start of the season, so they are very familiar with the track.

Barcelona, Spain

- **First held:** 1991
- **Length:** 4.7km (2.9 miles)
- **Laps:** 66 **Corners:** 16

Overpass

Suzuka is the only F1 circuit with a figure of eight layout. Cars return to the start/finish via an overpass.

Suzuka, Japan

- **First held:** 1987
- **Length:** 5.8km (3.6 miles)
- **Laps:** 53 **Corners:** 18

This section of track is shown in the photo below.

Tunnel

Monte Carlo, Monaco

- **First held:** 1929
- **Length:** 3.3km (2.1 miles)
- **Laps:** 78 **Corners:** 19

The skill needed to navigate the Monaco circuit, coupled with the glamorous location, make it a race F1 drivers dream of winning.

The Loews corner, named after the nearby hotel, is the slowest turn in F1 racing.

Barriers either side of the road mean crashes are more likely.

Around the track

Each year Grand Prix races are held at 17 to 19 different race tracks. Together they make up the F1 championship.

F1 champion

Around 12 teams take part in a championship. Each team has two drivers, who score points for finishing a race in the top eight. The driver with the most points is the champion.

Ferrari team driver Kimi Räikkönen takes part in the qualifying rounds for the first Abu Dhabi Grand Prix.

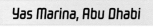

Yas Marina, Abu Dhabi

- **First held:** 2009
- **Circuit length:** 5.5km (3.4 miles)
- **Laps:** 55 **Corners:** 21

The racing line shows the ideal position of the car around the track, to give the fastest time.

Grandstands are positioned around the track to give spectators different views.

Run-off areas slow a car down if it comes off the track.

A chicane is an S-shaped bend in the track.

Pit lane where the driver pulls in for repairs or a new tyre.

The pit garages

A hotel has been built bridging over the track.

Yachts moor here in the Yas Marina.

The paddock is the area where teams set up their motorhome bases.

Drivers exit the pits via a tunnel.

This spectacular building is a hotel on the Yas Marina circuit in Abu Dhabi. The circuit was built in 2009.

Preparing for a race

Grand Prix races are held on Sundays, but teams arrive earlier in the week to set up, get ready and qualify for the race.

What each team needs:

- **People:** maximum 48
- **Racing cars:** 3
- **Spare chassis:** 1
- **Spare engines:** 2
- **Full set of other spares**
- **Tyres:** 18 sets of 4 per car per race weekend
- **Fuel:** 180-250 litres of petrol per car per race weekend

Car trucks transport the teams' cars and parts to the Grand Prix pit garages.

Each team sets up a luxurious motorhome base in the paddock area of the track.

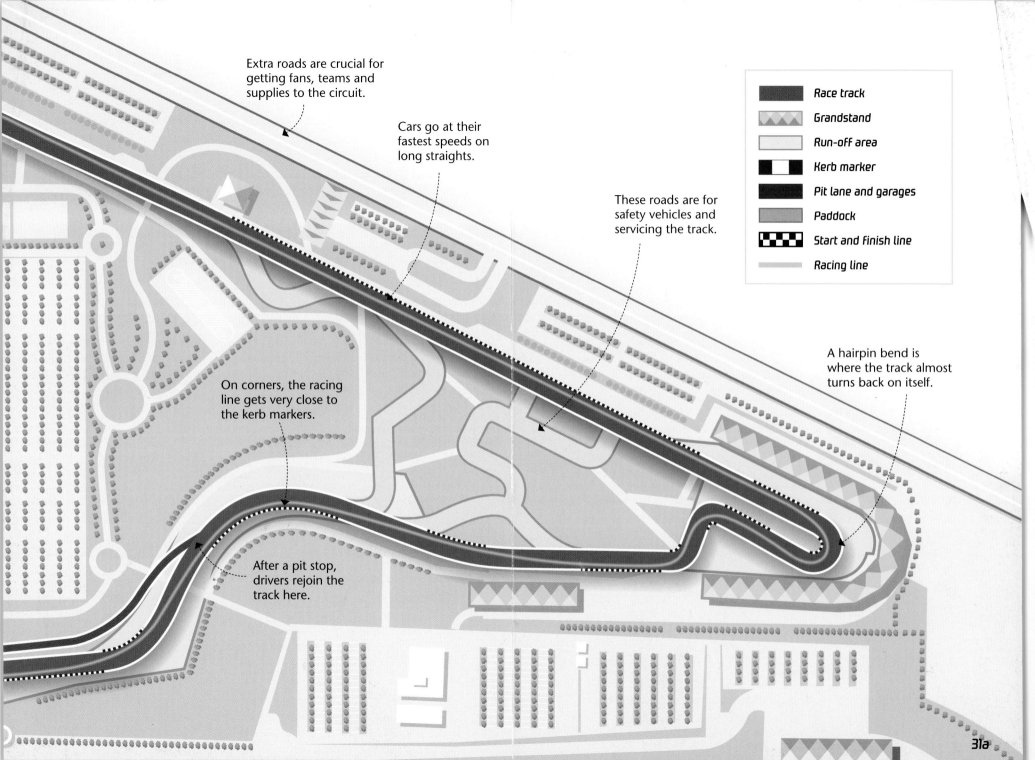

Extra roads are crucial for getting fans, teams and supplies to the circuit.

Cars go at their fastest speeds on long straights.

These roads are for safety vehicles and servicing the track.

A hairpin bend is where the track almost turns back on itself.

On corners, the racing line gets very close to the kerb markers.

After a pit stop, drivers rejoin the track here.

Race track	
Grandstand	
Run-off area	
Kerb marker	
Pit lane and garages	
Paddock	
Start and finish line	
Racing line	

Wednesday and Thursday

Drivers study the circuit closely, on foot or on scooters.

Mechanics assemble the racing cars and practise pit stops (see p38).

Friday

Teams test the cars on the track and make last-minute changes.

Drivers are available for pre-race interviews with the media.

Saturday, usually 2-3pm

FASTEST LAP

Drivers do three rounds of qualifying laps to decide the starting order for Sunday's race.

On the starting line

The start of a Grand Prix race is a spectacular sight. Around 20 cars are staggered on the starting grid, engines roaring, heat rising and crowds cheering.

Waiting for the start of the Chinese F1 Grand Prix in 2007

Mechanic

Start lights

Ready	●	●	●	○	○
Steady	●	●	●	●	●
Go	○	○	○	○	○

There are five red start lights. They light up one by one when the cars are ready. Then they all switch off together, signalling the race start.

Start/finish line

The pit wall, where the team manager and race engineers sit.

The pit lane

Cars line up in the places they have qualified for on the previous day.

Driving skills

Each race begins with a mad dash for the first corner. Drivers try to overtake, while defending their position from the car behind.

Cornering

The driver's approach to a corner is known as a line. It's important to get the line just right.

This diagram shows three different racing lines.

| Early | Ideal | Late |

The dots show the point in each line where the car starts to exit the corner, known as the apex.

Below you can see what happens to the blue, yellow and red cars as they exit the corner.

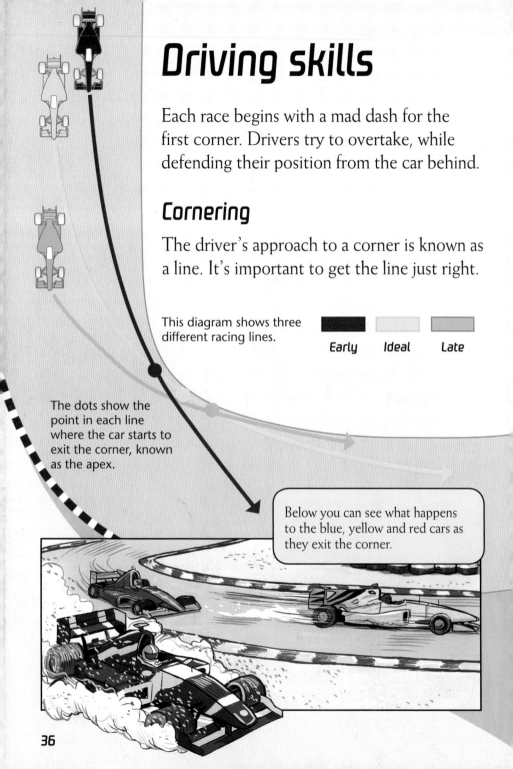

Slipstreams and overtaking

When a car travels fast, the disturbed air it creates behind it is known as a slipstream.

On straight stretches slipstreams suck in the car behind and help it to accelerate.

2
Blue pulls out and overtakes.

Run-off area

1
Blue uses Red's slipstream to accelerate.

But slipstreams also reduce downforce. On a corner cars need downforce to grip the track.

Orange's slipstream is reducing Green's downforce.

1

Green needs to slow down to keep control round the corner...

Kerb marker

2

...so Orange races away.

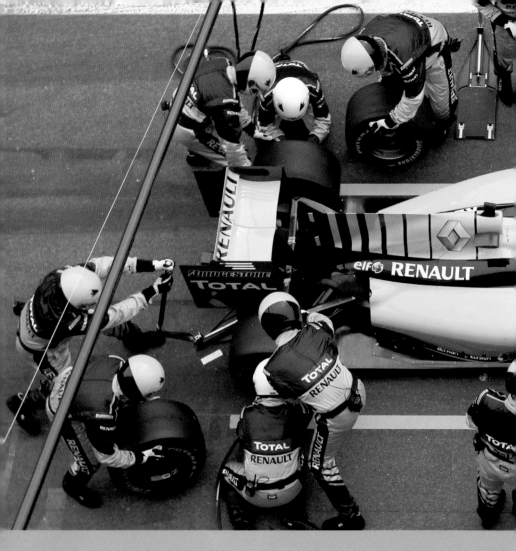

Pit stops

During a race, cars make pit stops for new tyres, repairs or mechanical adjustments, all in under five seconds. From 1994 to 2009 cars used to refuel as well. Precious time can be lost at pit stops, so the crews practise hundreds of times.

A Renault makes a pit stop in the Spanish Grand Prix, 2010.

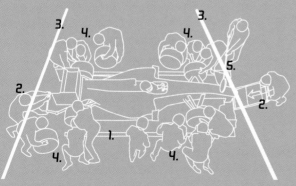

1. Lines mark exact position for car to stop.
2. Car is raised at front and back.
3. Two tubes carry wires for pneumatic wrenches.
4. Three mechanics change each wheel, using wrench.
5. 'Lollipop' man signals stop and go.

A Red Bull car hits the crash barrier during the Australian Grand Prix in 2006.

The car was destroyed, but the driver walked away unharmed.

Accidents happen

With over 20 cars zooming around a track at top speed, accidents do happen. But strict safety rules and rapid emergency responses mean drivers are rarely seriously injured.

Survival cell

F1 car designs have to pass 15 crash tests. The car body may crumple, but the survival cell where the driver sits has to remain intact.

Emergency help at a Grand Prix

- **Fire engines:** 5, each with 4 firefighters
- **Helicopters:** 2, one with a doctor aboard
- **Ambulances:** 4 along the race track
- **Salvage cars:** 4, carrying rescue cutters and fire extinguishers
- **Rescue cars:** 2, to transport medical staff
- **Medical centre:** 1 (as good as a hospital)

Michael Schumacher crosses the finish line, winning the European Grand Prix in 2006.

Slippery surface ahead	Mechanical problem – return to pit	Warning for unsporting behaviour	Car excluded from race – return to pit	Beware, slow vehicles on track

* These flags are accompanied by the number of the car in trouble.

Indy cars

In America, the main open-wheel racing cars are known as Indy cars. Their name comes from the Indianapolis 500 Mile Race, or Indy 500 for short, which has been going for over a hundred years.

Banking

Indy cars race mostly on oval circuits. The corners of the circuits slope up at an angle. This is known as banking. The steeper the banking, the faster the cars can go.

The IndyCar Series has up to 19 races each year. They take place mainly in the USA but also in Canada, Japan and Brazil.

Indy versus F1 - what's the difference?

Indy

- **Spec cars:** All chassis and engines are made to the same specifications by the same manufacturers.

- **Mostly oval circuits:** On the long straights and banked corners, Indy cars reach higher speeds than F1 cars.

Formula One

- **Open formula cars:** Within the formula rules, each team can design their own car parts.

- **No oval circuits:** Each F1 circuit is different. Drivers need expert cornering skills and knowledge of the track.

Here Danica Patrick, one of the few female racing drivers, leads the way at the Indy 500.

Indy 500

The Indy 500 takes place in May on the Indianapolis Motor Speedway, the first purpose-built US track.

■	Race track
☐	Grandstands
☐	Spectator mounds
■	Garages
▦	Start and finish line

Indianapolis Motor Speedway

- **Built in:** 1909
- **Circuit length:** 4km (2.5 miles)
- **Laps:** 200 for Indy 500
- **Banking:** 9°

There's seating on mounds inside the track.

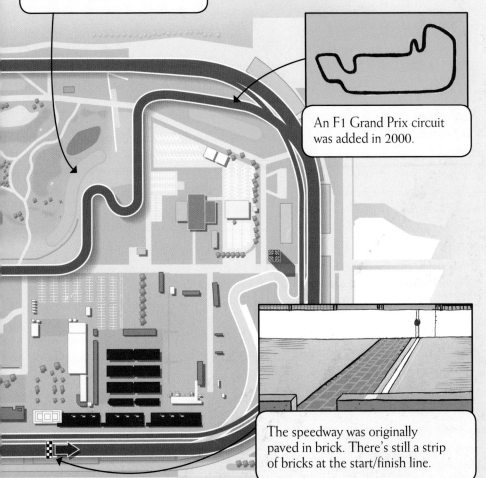

An F1 Grand Prix circuit was added in 2000.

The speedway was originally paved in brick. There's still a strip of bricks at the start/finish line.

Stock cars

Early stock cars were just normal road vehicles, but over the years modifications have been introduced to improve their speed and safety.

No. 42 Target Chevrolet, 2010

- **Top speed:** 320km/h (200mph)
- **Engine:** V8, 850hp
- **0-100km/h (0-62mph):** 4s

Roof flaps open if the car spins out of control. They cut through the air flow and stop the car from flipping over.

Strong steel-tubed frame including roll cage surrounds the driver.

Safety harness

Shatterproof windscreen

Engine, 4 times as powerful as a normal car's

Slick tyres filled with nitrogen

Main tyre

Inner liner – a tyre inside the main tyre

Inner liner
On longer tracks tyres must have an inner liner. If the main tyre bursts, the driver can still slow down safely.

1,879mm (74 inches)

5,290mm (208.25 inches)

Grills to cool the engine

Oval tracks

Stock cars mostly race on oval tracks. The tracks come in three different categories, according to length. The design of the car depends on the length of track it's racing on.

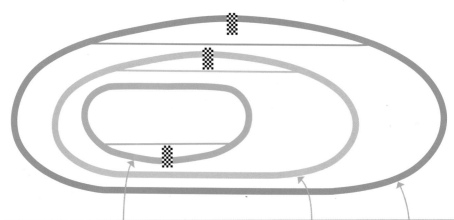

	Short track	Speedway	Superspeedway
Track details	• Under 1.6km (1 mile) • Frequent turns • Short straights	• 1.6km-3.2km (1-2 miles) • Less frequent turns • Longer straights	• Over 3.2km (2 miles) • Infrequent turns • Very long straights
Design priority	• Creating downforce	• Creating downforce	• Reducing drag
Design solutions	• Car slanted, nose to left, tail to right • Back raised so rear wing catches more air		• Car body very straight and low
Other differences	• Grill openings enlarged to help air cool engine	• Small grill openings (airflow at higher speed is sufficient to cool engine)	• Engine is restricted to 450hp so the car can't go dangerously fast

Pack racing

On steep-banked corners stock cars race in a large pack. The slipstreams from the cars ahead make them go faster.

Bump and run

Stock cars are allowed to bump each other. Here the purple car nudges the orange one.

While the orange car regains control, the purple one sneaks past and overtakes.

Daytona International Speedway

In the early 1900s, drivers used to race on the hard sand of Daytona Beach in Florida, USA. Then the Daytona International Speedway was built. It hosts several famous stock car races, including the Daytona 500.

The Coke Zero 400 is a 400-mile stock car night race. It takes place at Daytona every year on the first Saturday in July.

Daytona International Speedway

- **First held:** 1959
- **Circuit length:** 4km (2.5 miles)
- **Laps:** 200 for Daytona 500, 160 for Coke Zero 400
- **Banking:** 18° at start/finish, 31° on other corners

The speedway shape is tri-oval. The triangle part gives spectators better views.

Start/Finish	
Race track	
Pit lane	
Direction	

Rally cars

Rally cars don't race together. They leave at set intervals and their times are recorded. The car with the fastest time wins.

Ford Focus RS WRC, 2010

- **Top speed:** 205km/h (127mph)
- **Engine:** 4 cylinder, 300hp
- **0–100km/h (0–62mph):** 3.6s

Rally cars drive on all surfaces and in all conditions. This Ford car has a turbocharged engine and four-wheel drive.

World Rally Championship (WRC)

The WRC consists of 13 three-day rallies held around the world. Each rally is divided into 15-35 stages of varying distances.

Rally timetable	
Preparation	
Tuesday and Wednesday	• Teams drive through the stages and take notes.
Thursday	• Teams test the cars on a practice stage, called a shakedown.
The competition	
Friday to Sunday	• Cars start each stage at 1-2 minute intervals. • Their times are recorded for each stage and added up. • Teams drive from one stage to the next on public roads. • Service parks are set up on the way for car repairs/maintenance. • The cars are kept in a secure area overnight.

Rally tactics

Rally cars have a driver and a co-driver. In many rallies they are allowed to drive through the course before the competition, so they know what's coming next.

Pacenotes

The co-driver takes notes, called pacenotes, then reads them to the driver during the race.

Pacenotes are usually written in shorthand like this:

70   3L -> 60 -> ! J

150   1R bmp   2L

SqR 50   2L

2L Cr   130   3R J

30   4R K -> ! J F

! 1L K F -> !!J   45

How to read pacenotes

number on its own: distance in metres

numbers 1-5 before R or L : speed for bend (1 = slowest)

R: right

L: left

bmp: bump

K: kink

J: jump

!: caution

->: into

Cr: crest

Sq: square / 90°

F: flat

Handbrake turn

To move quickly round a tight bend, rally drivers often use the handbrake.

One left!

While driving at speed, the driver yanks up the handbrake which locks the rear wheels.

The car slides to the side, helping the driver to turn the corner more quickly.

Hill jumping

Spectators and drivers love a good hill jump. The driver zooms up the hill at top speed. As he reaches the crest, the car keeps going up... before landing with a bump.

Sports cars

Sports cars are specially designed for long-distance, endurance racing, so they have to be reliable and efficient, as well as fast. There are two main categories: grand tourers (GTs) and sports prototypes.

Grand tourers

GTs are based on ordinary cars, but everything inside is highly modified to make the cars more powerful.

Rear wing

Maserati MC12, 2010

- **Top speed:** 330km/h (205mph)
- **Engine:** V12, 600hp
- **0-100km/h (0-62mph):** 3.7s

GT cars all have closed cockpits.

Yellow headlights

Enclosed wheels

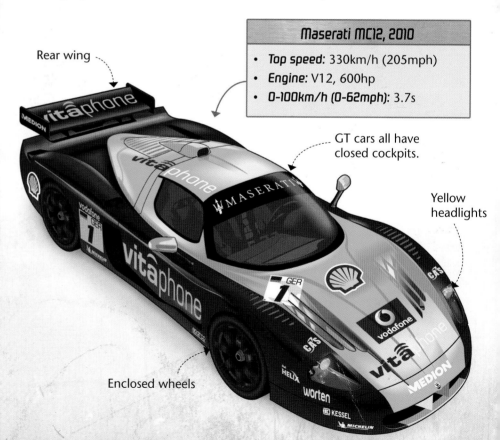

The Le Mans pit lane

Every year around 50 cars compete in the 24 Hours of Le Mans race. The hub of the action is the pit lane, where mechanics hover while excited spectators look on.

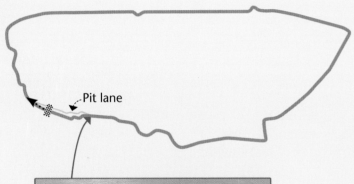

Pit lane

Le Mans, France

- **First held:** 1923
- **Circuit length:** 13.6km (8.5 miles)
- **Laps:** as many as possible in 24 hours
- **Track:** permanent road course and temporarily closed off public roads

Testing technology

The 24-hour race started off as an endurance test for ordinary cars. Today, new technologies are often tested first in Le Mans sports cars.

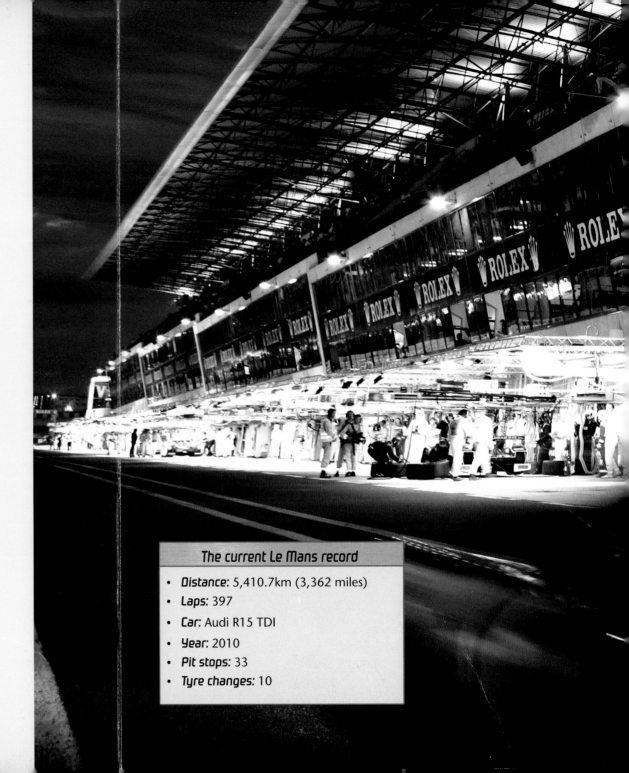

The current Le Mans record

- **Distance:** 5,410.7km (3,362 miles)
- **Laps:** 397
- **Car:** Audi R15 TDI
- **Year:** 2010
- **Pit stops:** 33
- **Tyre changes:** 10

Sports prototypes

These are purpose-built racing cars, with either an open or closed cockpit.

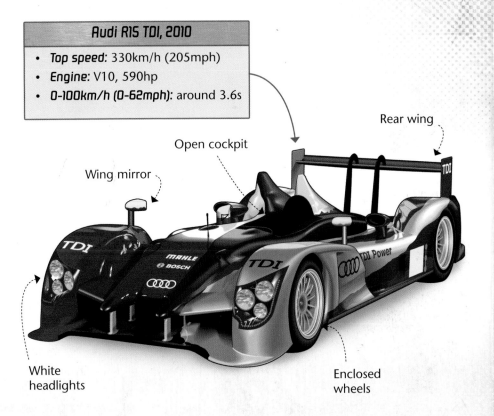

Audi R15 TDI, 2010
• **Top speed:** 330km/h (205mph)
• **Engine:** V10, 590hp
• **0-100km/h (0-62mph):** around 3.6s

Rear wing

Open cockpit

Wing mirror

White headlights

Enclosed wheels

24 hours of Le Mans

The oldest and most famous sports car race takes place in Le Mans, France, in June each year. Two classes of prototypes and two classes of GTs all compete to cover the furthest distance over 24 hours.

Dragsters

Dragsters compete in short, straight sprint races. Two cars race at a time and the winner goes through to the next round. The fastest class of drag racing is top fuel.

Al-Anabi top fuel, 2010
• **Top speed:** 530km/h (330mph)
• **Engine:** V8, 7,000hp
• **0-160km/h (0-100mph):** 0.9s

The rear wing creates downforce to keep the wheels on the track.

The fuel contains up to 90% nitromethane which makes it very powerful.

Each car has a team of three drivers. Two watch and wait their turn while the other one races.

Each team has its own pit garage, where mechanics wait through night and day to make both emergency and scheduled changes.

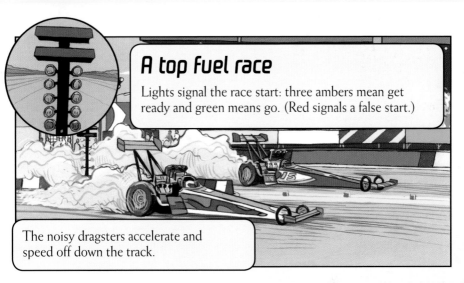

A top fuel race

Lights signal the race start: three ambers mean get ready and green means go. (Red signals a false start.)

The noisy dragsters accelerate and speed off down the track.

Dragsters travel so fast they need parachutes to slow them down after they've crossed the finish line.

A top fuel dragster accelerates faster than any other vehicle on land.

The fastest cars... ever

The fastest cars of all are designed to set new land speed records. The first car to exceed 1,000km/h (620mph) was the Blue Flame in 1970. The current record is held by Thrust SSC, the first car to go faster than the speed of sound.

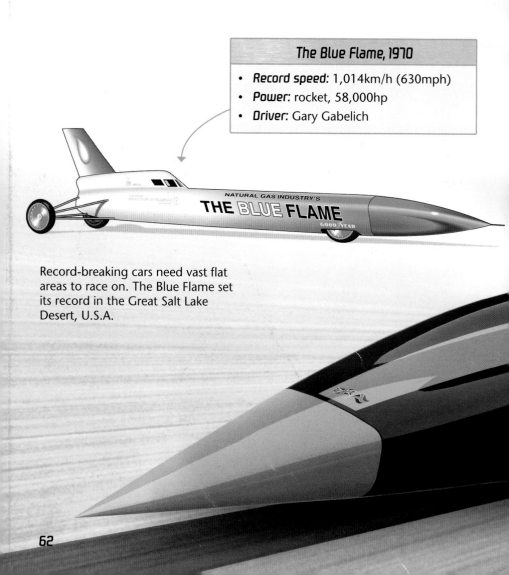

The Blue Flame, 1970

- **Record speed:** 1,014km/h (630mph)
- **Power:** rocket, 58,000hp
- **Driver:** Gary Gabelich

Record-breaking cars need vast flat areas to race on. The Blue Flame set its record in the Great Salt Lake Desert, U.S.A.

Thrust SSC's engines are the same as the ones used in jet fighter planes.

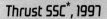

Thrust SSC*, 1997

- **Record speed:** 1,228km/h (763mph)
- **Engines:** 2 turbofans, 110,000hp
- **Driver:** Andy Green

*SSC stands for "supersonic car", which means it's faster than the speed of sound.

The team behind Thrust SSC is now designing a new car, Bloodhound SSC. They hope it will set a new land speed record of over 1,600km/h (1,000mph).

An artist's impression of Bloodhound SSC

Saving energy

A racing car can burn up 100 litres of fuel in just one race. One of the greatest challenges to manufacturers is how to make cars more energy efficient. Solar power and electricity are now being tried out as alternatives.

Solar cars

Tokai Challenger, 2009

- **Top speed:** 94km/h (58mph)
- **Power:** 6m² of solar panels, motor
- **Race:** winner of 2009 World Solar Challenge – 3,000km (1,864 miles) across Australia

The surface of the car is covered in solar panels, to capture as much sunlight as possible.

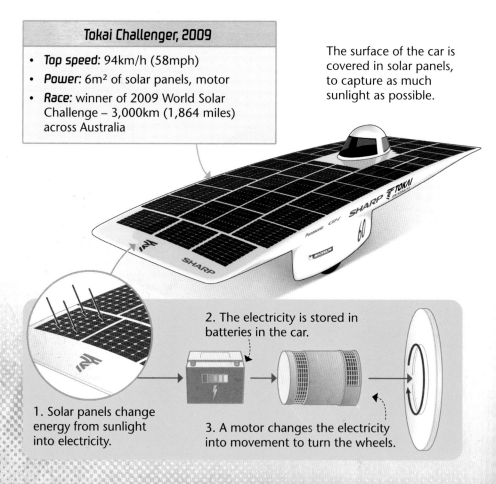

1. Solar panels change energy from sunlight into electricity.

2. The electricity is stored in batteries in the car.

3. A motor changes the electricity into movement to turn the wheels.

Electric cars

Like solar cars, electric ones use electricity to run motors which turn the cars' wheels.

ALPHA 1 SRF*, 2010

- **Top speed:** 230km/h (155mph)
- **Power:** electricity and 2 motors, each 180hp
- **Race:** international electric races

*SRF stands for "Silent Radical Force".

The car charges up with electricity through this plug socket.

Hybrid electric

Hybrid cars can run on either electricity through a motor or fuel through an engine.

Porsche 911 GT3 R, 2010

- **Top speed:** 306km/h (190mph)
- **Power:** 2 motors, each 82hp, plus rear flat-6 engine, 680hp
- **Race:** 12-24 hour endurance races

The car charges up with electricity when the engine is running.

Racing back in time

The first major car race took place in France in 1895. It ran from Paris to Bordeaux and back again, and the winner was French car manufacturer Emile Levassor.

Panhard and Levassor, 1895

- **Top speed:** 25km/h (15.5mph)
- **Engine power:** 4hp

Levassor took nearly 49 hours to travel 1,178km (732 miles).

In the USA, Henry Ford collaborated with a bicycle racer to construct two racing cars, the 999s.

Ford 999, 1902

- **Top speed:** 146km/h (91mph)
- **Engine power:** 80hp

The 999s won many races and one briefly held the land speed record.

Marcel Renault's racing car was one of many to crash in the Paris to Madrid race of 1903. Eight people died. After that, open road racing was banned in France.

Renault, 1903

- **Top speed:** around 130km/h (80mph)
- **Engine power:** 40hp

Marcel was a co-founder of Renault cars. He died from his injuries in the 1903 crash.

US racing driver Barney Oldfield collaborated with car builder Harry Miller to design a safer racing car. It was the first racing car to feature an enclosed cockpit.

Miller Golden Submarine, 1917

- **Top speed:** 177km/h (110mph)
- **Engine power:** 136hp

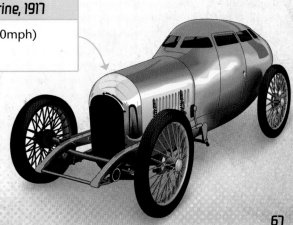

The Golden Submarine competed in 54 races and won 20.

Brooklands enabled thousands of spectators to enjoy races in safety for the first time.

The first tracks

The first tracks used for car racing were oval horse racing tracks in the USA. The first purpose-built track, Brooklands, was constructed in England in 1907.

Brooklands, England

- **Races held:** 1907-1938
- **Circuit length:** 5.2km (3.3 miles)
- **Banking:** 30°
- **Surface:** concrete

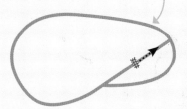

It was followed two years later by America's Indianapolis Motor Speedway.

Hall of fame

Here are some of the top racing drivers over the years, across the different types of races.

Motorsport	Driver	Titles	Famous for
Formula One	**Ayrton Senna** 1960-1994 Brazilian	F1 champion 3 times	Amazing wet weather skills. Killed in Grand Prix crash in Italy.
	Michael Schumacher Born in 1969 German	F1 champion 7 times	Best F1 record ever. Returned to F1 from retirement in 2010.
Indy racing (formerly known as Champ car)	**A.J. Foyt** Born in 1935 American	IndyCar series champion 7 times	Also won 3 stock car championships and the 24 hours of Le Mans.
	Danica Patrick Born in 1982 American	Won the Indy Japan 300 in 2008	First woman to win an Indy car race.
Stock car racing	**Richard Petty** Born in 1937 American	National Association of Stock Car Auto Racing (NASCAR) champion 7 times	Long racing career (1,184 races over 35 years).
	Dale Earnhardt 1951-2001 American	NASCAR champion 7 times	Aggressive racing style. Killed in a Daytona 500 race.

Motorsport	Driver	Titles	Famous for
Rallying	**Sebastien Loeb** Born in 1974 French	World Rally champion 7 times	Most wins in the World Rally Championship.
Sports car racing	**Tom Kristensen** Born in 1967 Danish	Won 24 Hours of Le Mans 8 times and 12 Hours of Sebring 5 times	Most wins at Le Mans.
Drag racing	**Tony Schumacher** Born in 1969 American	National Hot Rod Association (NHRA) Top Fuel champion 7 times	First NHRA driver to exceed 530 km/h (330 mph).

Triple crown

The only driver ever to win the Monaco Grand Prix, Indy 500 and 24 Hours of Le Mans is Graham Hill. This achievement is known as the triple crown.

Graham Hill
1929-1975
British

Graham Hill performs a victory lap at Monaco in 1969.

How to become an F1 racing driver

It takes talent, luck and years of practice to race at the highest levels. Most drivers start training by the age of 10.

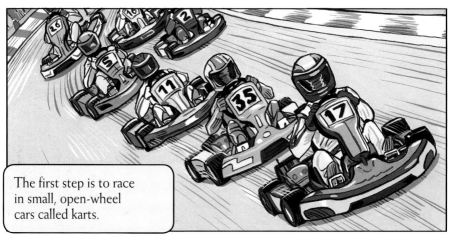

The first step is to race in small, open-wheel cars called karts.

Keep Fit

Fitness and stamina are essential. Go running, swimming or cycling and try some weight-lifting.

Strengthen up

Weights attached to helmet

Driver pulls against weights

Racing at top speed puts the upper body under great pressure, so you'll need to do special neck exercises.

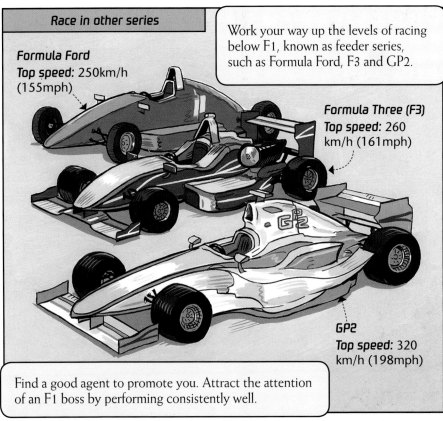

Race in other series

Work your way up the levels of racing below F1, known as feeder series, such as Formula Ford, F3 and GP2.

Formula Ford
Top speed: 250km/h (155mph)

Formula Three (F3)
Top speed: 260 km/h (161mph)

GP2
Top speed: 320 km/h (198mph)

Find a good agent to promote you. Attract the attention of an F1 boss by performing consistently well.

Become an F1 test driver, get your 'Super Licence', then get picked to race for your team.

If you win the most points across the season, you'll become World Champion.

Thousands of excited fans watch a 2006 stock car race at the Talladega Superspeedway, USA.

Racing cars on the internet

There are lots of websites with information about racing cars. At the Usborne Quicklinks website you'll find links to some great sites where you can:

- find out who's winning in this year's championships
- take a virtual drive through the Grand Prix race tracks
- learn more about how stock cars work
- read up on the history of motor racing

For links to these sites and more go to the Usborne Quicklinks website at www.usborne.com/quicklinks and enter the keywords **racing cars**.

Glossary

The glossary explains some of the words used in this book.

brake caliper Two arms that squeeze together to slow down the brake disc in a wheel.

carbon fibre A light, incredibly strong material made out of extremely thin fibres.

chassis The main framework of a car. In F1 cars, the carbon fibre body is included in the chassis.

crankshaft The part of an engine that turns the sideways motion of the pistons into rotation.

downforce The downward pressure created by the wings on a car as it passes through the air.

drag The resistance caused by the air as a car travels at speed.

dragster A car that competes in a short, straight race known as a drag race.

drive shaft A rod that connects the gear box with the wheels.

exhaust Pipes that guide gases produced by the engine away from the car.

flat-6 An engine with six cylinders arranged horizontally.

fuel injection A system for adding a precise mixture of fuel and air to the engine.

gears Toothed machine parts that interlock and rotate. They are used to change speed or direction.

groove An indented line on a tyre.

kart A small open-wheel car, used as an introduction to motor racing.

KERS Kinetic Energy Recovery System, a device used to capture and reuse energy that's normally lost when a car brakes.

lap Once round a track or circuit. If a car is ahead of another by one or more complete circuits, it is said to lap the other car.

NASCAR The National Association for Stock Car Auto Racing, governs some of the main stock car racing series in America.

paddock The area of a race track where teams set up temporary bases.

piston A solid cylinder in a brake or engine system that moves back and forth to transfer motion.

pit lane Part of a circuit where cars can stop for mechanics to make changes.

pneumatic wrench A tool powered by pressurised gas, used to remove and replace a tyre.

rallying A competition where cars drive from point to point and their times are recorded.

road course Any purpose-built race track that's not an oval.

service park An area in a rally designated for car maintenance. Spectators are allowed access to see the cars.

sidepod Bodywork on the side of a car that covers the radiators and engine exhaust.

slick A smooth-surfaced tyre.

slipstream The turbulent air behind a car when it travels fast.

starting grid A marked section of a track at the start, where cars line up according to their qualifying times, with the fastest at the front.

straight A straight section of a race track.

streamlined Designed with smooth sides to create the least resistance.

street circuit A temporary race course on streets closed off to the public.

survival cell The super-strong central section of a car that protects the driver in a crash.

test bed A secure platform for rigorous testing of large items, such as an engine.

tread A pattern of grooves on a tyre, particularly useful in wet conditions.

turbocharger A gas compressor that forces more air into the engine to create more power.

turbofan A jet engine with a fan that brings in more air and creates extra thrust.

wind tunnel A big room used for testing cars. It has a massive fan that replicates the air pressure on a car travelling at top speed.

Index

Page numbers marked with an 'a' are found underneath the flap on that page.

Acknowledgements

Every effort has been made to trace and acknowledge ownership of copyright. If any rights have been omitted, the publishers offer to rectify this in any future editions following notification. The publishers are grateful to the following individuals and organizations for their permission to reproduce material on the following pages:

cover © REUTERS/Heino Kalis/Action Images; **p2-3** © George Tiedemann/GT Images/Corbis; **p14-15** © Jon Feingersh/Stone/Getty Images; **p18-19** © REUTERS/Alessandro Garofalo/Action Images; **p22** © Schlegelmilch/Corbis; **p28-29** © Peter Van Egmond/Action Images; **p30-31** © Peter Steffen/epa/Corbis; **p34-35** © Michael Reynolds/epa/Corbis; **p38-39** © Andrew Ferraro/LAT Photographic; **p40-41** © Steven Tee/LAT Photographic; **p42-43** Roland Weihrauch/epa/Corbis; **p44-45** © William Manning/Corbis; **p52-53** © Worth Canoy/Icon SMI/Corbis; **p54-55** McKlein (image supplied courtesy of Ford); **p58a-59a** © Michael Haegele/Corbis; **p60-61** © David Allio/Icon SMI/Corbis; **p62-63** BLOODHOUND SSC; **p69** © Schlegelmilch/Corbis; **p72-73** The Brooklands Society; **p74-75** © George Tiedemann/GT Images/Corbis

Car and map illustrations p4, 5, 6, 7, 8, 9, 10a-11a, 30a-31a, 38-39, 44-45, 58, 59, 62, 63, 64, 65, 66, 67 © Adrian Dean/F1ARTWORK

F1, FORMULA ONE and GRAND PRIX are trade marks of Formula One Licensing BV, a Formula One Group Company. NASCAR® is a registered trade mark of the National Association for Stock Car Auto Racing, Inc. Indy 500 and IndyCar are registered trade marks of Brickyard Trademarks, Inc.

Thanks for additional research material to:
Nicola Armstrong and Bastien Hibon at
MERCEDES GP PETRONAS Formula One Team
Emma Ecob at Williams F1
Billy Curwood at Earnhardt Ganassi

Series editor: Jane Chisholm Series designer: Zoe Wray
Digital design: Nick Wakeford and John Russell